HEAR AND NOW

Lara Foot Newton & Lionel Newton

HEAR AND NOW

OBERON BOOKS
LONDON

First published in 2006 by Oberon Books Ltd
521 Caledonian Road, London N7 9RH
Tel: 020 7607 3637 / Fax: 020 7607 3629
e-mail: info@oberonbooks.com
www.oberonbooks.com

A catalogue record for this book is available from the British Library.

ISBN: 1 84002 675 8

Cover image by Gerhard Marx

Notes on design

The floor is a series of deep grey front-doors, laid flat on the ground and at a slight angle to the audience. Closer inspection reveals that this could be the two-storey façade of an apartment complex. Upstage, two of the doors are raised from floor level, propped up by a collection of books embedded in earth to resemble archaeological strata. Other collections of books are scattered informally across the space. On one of the raised levels, upstage-right, we find a small-scale bed, untidy and strewn with books seemingly in the process of being read. The other raised surface, upstage-left, has various items scattered across it, leaving the impression that it is used as table. Upstage, behind all this, is an array of ladders of various sizes. These dark-coloured household ladders have been adapted for various functions: the tallest has a strange growth on one of its legs, a primitive string-instrument has been grafted onto it; the other ladders host a contraption which provides subtitles; another ladder provides domestic shelving. The effect is of a musty, hermetic apartment interior, inhabited by a lonely man obsessed with books, literature and fictions, overlaid onto the site of an archaeological excavation.

The main character, the inhabitant of this space, is crippled; his appearance is strange, disproportioned. A set of wooden legs, the size of a young child's, are strapped around his waist. The actor moves around on his knees, using crutches as support, leaving the useless wooden legs dangling from his waist. Visually, he is a hybrid: a combination of wooden prosthetic childhood legs coupled with equally dysfunctional adult legs. Using his crutches, he moves around with difficulty, a man dragging with him the lame legs of a boy, smoking and reading compulsively, as if to escape his physical predicament.

Other architectural features also make reference to medical prosthetics. A small steel window lies useless on the floor with curious handles protruding from its base – until the man picks it up, swings it into position and looks out onto the world outside. In similar manner, the female character (the woman next door) is associated with the front door to his apartment. This door, of a size that covers the torso and head when held upright, has a single aluminium leg – a sort of crutch protruding from its frame. This door, the entrance to his world, is mobile in a similar manner to the window. The woman carries the door like a suitcase, swings it onto the crutch-leg and knocks. She opens the door to peep into his world, and when let in, it is through this door that she gains access to his claustrophobic world. When not in use, these architectural 'prostheses' are scattered around him like the debris of a natural disaster.

What should also be noted is how the 'sound', the cry referred to by the characters, is produced. The ladder with the string instrument grafted onto it is not only a hybrid of ladder and instrument but also a mix of traditional African string-instrument and cello: a cello string is strung over a calabash, which acts as sound-box. The sound, a continuous wailing, is not produced by this string, but when the actress runs her fingers over a thin piece of string attached to it.

During the final scenes of the play, the man lifts or opens some of the doors, the floor-panels of his apartment. Opening the doors reveals earth beneath them and allows for the burying of objects as referred to in the text. With objects buried beneath them, the half-closed doors add to the image of exposed archeological strata, the mangled histories in which they live their lives.

Gerhard Marx
Designer

Characters

MAN, early forties

WOMAN, late forties

Hear and Now was first performed in June 2005 at The State Theatre, Pretoria, and had its British premiere at the Gate Theatre, London, on 30 May 2006 with the following company:

MAN, Lionel Newton

WOMAN, Denise Newman

Directors, Lara Foot Newton & Gerhard Marx

Designer, Gerhard Marx

Lighting Designer, Wesley France

Stage Manager, Marisa Steenkamp

Produced by duckrabbit in association with The State Theatre, Pretoria

Hear and Now was inspired by a series of sketches by Gerhard Marx in response to short stories by Jan Rabie, and later developed in a number of image and ideas workshops with Tony Hamburger, Maja Marx, Denise Newman and Wesley France.

Special thanks to Aubrey Sekhabi, The Baxter Theatre, Sir Peter Hall, Rolex, Malcolm Purkey, David Peimer, Mark Fleishman, Regina Seebright, The National Lottery – South Africa, The Market Theatre and The NAC.

Hear and Now

A soft, warm light, slowly reveals the face of a WOMAN,
and the silhouette of a buckled MAN.

WOMAN

There are many ways of loving,

I sit comforted by my usefulness,

Counting the ways of loving, I wonder at my lack of
choice.

Like pieces of a puzzle, he and I have our place.

He malformed buckled bowed. His room an island,
isolated floating – an abandoned library – books line
the walls, and a jarring door, intruding, reminding
him of the outside world.

> *Cross-fade to the room.*
>
> *The MAN is revealed.*
>
> *We see the buckled MAN. He walks over to a small*
> *table, lights a cigarette –*
>
> *He picks up the window, opens it and looks out,*
> *closes the window, puts it down.*
>
> *Opens it and mumbles to himself.*
>
> *Begins to read a book…*
>
> *Back to the window.*
>
> *Back to his book.*
>
> *There is a knock on the door.*

*The MAN picks up the door and opens it, sees the
WOMAN and shuts it angrily.*

The WOMAN opens the door.

MAN
Are you back?

WOMAN
Yes.

MAN
For how long?

WOMAN
As long as I can bear it.

MAN
Rather go now.

WOMAN
And leave you alone?

MAN
Yes.

Pause.

WOMAN
Did you wash the pots?

MAN
They're not my pots.

WOMAN
Of course they are your pots.

MAN
You bought them.

WOMAN
Yes. But for your house!
Pause.
Well did you wash them?

MAN
No.

Pause.

WOMAN
And the magazines? Did you read them?

MAN
What for?

WOMAN
For some light entertainment, you can't sit with this crap all day.

MAN

It's not crap. Maybe the owner will come back and take them. Maybe that will make you happy.

WOMAN

I even think you made that up; I even think these books are a lie.

MAN

Ja, ja...

WOMAN

And there is no rot, no sinking. You made that up too. I know, I found...

Are you hungry?

MAN

The earth turned slowly to mud...

WOMAN

Another book, another story.

MAN

Under God's Blanket, and then another blanket and another and another...

WOMAN

How did you breathe?

MAN

Periscope pipe.

WOMAN
And now? Where are you now?

MAN
Here.

WOMAN
Above ground?

MAN
Yes!

WOMAN
Why did it happen?

MAN
I've told you a thousand times! You just don't listen.
Pause. He watches her carefully.
Did you scatter her ashes?

WOMAN
No. I don't think I did.

MAN
You did, or you didn't?

WOMAN
I didn't.

Pause.

MAN

You said you were going to.

WOMAN

I counted the ducks.

MAN

And?

WOMAN

Eight!

MAN

Eight! Eight? Soon there will be none!

WOMAN

I know…

MAN

Two weeks ago it was down to nineteen, that's eleven ducks in two weeks. Five and a half ducks a week. The bloody hobos are eating the ducks!

WOMAN

How do you know it's the hobos?

MAN

Don't you read…?

WOMAN

It's another one of Skrewf's stories.

MAN

You leave Bra Skrewf out of this. You scatter your mother's ashes in the pond and you know what's going to happen. The tadpoles are going eat the ashes, the fish are going eat the tadpoles, the ducks are going to eat the fish, the hobos are going eat the ducks, and then some hobo is going to defecate outside my window, you're on your way to the supermarket, you walk out the door, slip in your mother, land on your elbow, you break your coccyx, and then you have to go up to your mother's flat, and use one of her old drips and stick it in your tit!

She can't help a smile.

WOMAN

The strangest thing happened to me yesterday.

MAN

Ja?

WOMAN

I was sitting at a coffee shop.

MAN

With who?

WOMAN

On my own. A coffee with cream on top.

MAN
Oh.

WOMAN
And this old woman comes in. She's got this dog-like energy. Panting and growling.

MAN
Growling?

WOMAN
She's got long fingers, painted nails, and a long coat. She sits down opposite me, takes my coffee, and drinks it all down.

MAN
Did she leave you any?

WOMAN
No.

MAN
What did you say?

WOMAN
Nothing.

MAN
Nothing? Well, what did you do?

WOMAN
Nothing.

MAN
Nothing?

WOMAN
I was terrified. She reminded me of someone.

MAN
Who?

WOMAN
I don't know…

MAN
Did she have a long nose?

WOMAN
Kind of…

MAN
Blue eyes?

WOMAN
I think so.

MAN
Kind of reddish hair?

WOMAN
I didn't see.

MAN
Did she have the hiccups?

WOMAN
What?

MAN
It's the pigeon lady!

WOMAN
Hey?

MAN
It's the pigeon lady! She's there every Friday at four,
she feeds the pigeons. She goes to Checkers, buys a
loaf of bread, breaks it up, throws it in the air, and
feeds the pigeons. Bra Skrewf says she's had the
hiccups for four years.

WOMAN
Four years? How?

MAN
According to Bra Skrewf she got a hell of a fright!
She was feeding the pigeons one day and there was
this sick ruffled one, hobbling along, had a cough
or something. Out of the blue this huge pigeon flies
down and starts having…intercourse with it, then

flies off. Not a second later another pigeon flies down and starts…to fornicate with it, and flies off. By this stage the pigeon is coughing its heart out. With not a moment to spare, a third pigeon, comes down and…you know gives it the one two three, and flies off. The coughing pigeon takes one step, another step and falls down stone dead. Now what Bra Skrewf and I can't agree upon is whether they fucked the pigeon to death, or whether they seized the opportunity while there was still a period of incubation.

WOMAN
And what has this got to do with the hiccups?

MAN
Maybe she swallowed a feather!

WOMAN
My coffee lady didn't have hiccups.

MAN
Maybe it was her sister.

WOMAN (*Laughing.*)
I will never leave you.

MAN (*Ironically.*)
I know.

> *They laugh.*
> *Music.*

WOMAN (*To audience.*)

When he was a boy he came from a town of certainty. Church steeples, ploughed fields, cream cakes, cows and certainty. The people were proud of their town and everything in it. And while outsiders helped to build it, they remained outsiders.

MAN (*Speaking to WOMAN.*)

Everything had its place, if you teased a bee it would sting you and die. If you tied a piece of cotton to a beetle you had a toy for the whole afternoon. We were happy, safe, proud. 'Hey my boy? Every brick, every fence! We ploughed the fields, we tarred the roads.'

WOMAN

He came from a small family; quiet biscuitly mother, strong father and abiding sister. All filled with the same certainty. But the boy was never certain – the boy was restless.

MAN

Dad was huge, and hairy, very hairy. Sis used to tease him…'you are a monkey, you are a monkey…'
And if he was in a good mood he would chase after her…

WOMAN

Then one day, shortly after his sixth birthday, a horrible thing happened.

MAN

Six candles. Six.

As the WOMAN narrates she plays the 'instrument'.

WOMAN

He woke up one night, he had heard a sound.
Perhaps a cry, perhaps a moan. No, more troubled
than a moan. One thing that he knew, was that the
sound belonged to something or someone that was
afraid, like the shrill sound of wind in an empty
house.

MAN

Something was broken…or scared, or sore, or
something…

WOMAN

He was terrified and called for his father. His father
entered quietly into the room,

'What is it boy?' he asked.

'Listen,' said the boy, 'I can hear a cry, someone is
dying.'

'I hear nothing,' said the father, 'it must be a bad
dream.'

'No,' said the boy climbing out of bed, 'we need to
go and see!'

'You hear nothing!' said the father.

She stops playing the instrument.

There are many ways of loving.

Music.

Cross-fade to some time ago.

MAN looking out of the window.

MAN

Hey! That's not your dog!

Ah for God sakes!

Luister mevrou dis nie jou bliksemse hond nie.

The WOMAN picks up the door and moves down stage left.

She knocks loudly.

The MAN covers his legs with a blanket.

Yes.

The WOMAN opens the door.

Look, sorry…

WOMAN

It is my dog! I'm a dog walker. It is in my care between seven and eight every morning. So between seven and eight, it is my dog. So it is my dog when you shout at me.

She closes the door, he goes to lock it. She opens it and sees his legs, he is embarrassed and turns to cover himself. She peaks through the door.

I pick him up at six fifty-five from flat 207, and then we walk down Sixth Street towards the park. Or at

least I walk; he doesn't like to walk, so I carry him.
I'm not sure if it's because he is old or scared. But he
doesn't like to walk. I mean it's not like he's cripple
or anything.

Silence.

*The WOMAN enters the room still looking through
the door.*

We walk past the flower-sellers, past Shopright-
Checkers, then up the hill to Green Park.

When we get to the park, we walk around till seven
fifty-five and then I bring him home.

His owner, Mrs Smidt, always greets him with
a Romany cream and says, 'Did you enjoy your
walkie Alfonzo?' I've never told her…you know,
that Alfonzo doesn't have a walkie. That I do all the
walking and that my arms are quite sore because
he's rather heavy. And I'd also like a Romany
cream.

MAN

Could you pass me my blanket?

She puts down the door and passes him the blanket.
She looks around the room.

You carry the dog?

WOMAN

Yes!

MAN
Are you my neighbour?

WOMAN
Yes.

MAN
Thirty-four?
Do you also hear the noise? At night?

WOMAN
I hear number twenty-nine playing Frank Sinatra.

MAN
No, that's twenty-seven.

WOMAN
Twenty-seven! And I hear the goings on and the squeaky bed in…

MAN / WOMAN (*Together.*)
Thirty-six!

Pause.

WOMAN
Have you read all of these?

MAN
A hundred and twenty-seven times.

WOMAN
You must be clever.

Pause.

MAN
Do you like books?

WOMAN
Yes.

MAN
Which is your favorite?

WOMAN
I can't remember.

MAN
Oh.
Pause.
When I moved in, the books were already here.
Waiting for me.

WOMAN
That was lucky. What if someone comes back to claim them?

MAN
Do you think they will?
I keep an eye on them.

WOMAN
Then they are yours!

MAN
Exactly!

WOMAN
Do you live alone?

MAN
Yes. You?

WOMAN
With my Mom, she's not very well... And your
family?

MAN
Dead.

WOMAN
I'm sorry... How did they...?

MAN
The town, where we lived, it sank one day.

WOMAN
Sank?

MAN
It was... It was a hot day, we were all crammed
into the old Ford. We stopped off at a petrol station,

the petrol attendant was smoking and I wondered whether he was going to set the car alight. Then my Mom…ah… Never mind… There was a tragedy, the town sank into the mud.

WOMAN
The mud?

MAN
It was a big…fuck up!

WOMAN
But you're ok?

MAN
I'm fine.

Music.

WOMAN (*To audience.*)
His father entered quietly into his room, 'What is it boy?' he asked.
Visual of legs.
The MAN manipulates the puppet legs, which are now detached from his body.
…as the boy stepped onto the floor his legs gave way, they crumpled like spaghetti under his weight.

MAN (*Playing his father.*)
'Stand up. Stand up!'

Visual as father carries the boy to the small bed.
Father / son imagery.

He once again attaches the legs to his body and
becomes the crippled MAN.

Cross-fade.

MAN with tea-cup in his mouth, WOMAN sitting.
She takes the tea.

WOMAN
Thank you.

MAN surprises her with Romany Creams.

MAN
Da dad a laaaa! BRRRRRRRRRRRRRRDISH!

WOMAN
Ha. My favorite. Did you go buy them especially for
me?

MAN
I sent Skrewf. That's why there're two missing. He
charges commission.

WOMAN
Skrewf?

MAN
Friend of mine – keeps me informed.

WOMAN
I brought you something too.
Da da laaa! BRRRRRRRRRRRRRDISH!

She gives him a gift. He opens it carefully.

MAN
A book? Thank you.
'The art of Rugby Tackling'.

WOMAN
I hope you haven't read it?

MAN
No… Not yet.

WOMAN
All the men in my family loved rugby. Yours?

MAN
My dad didn't really play but, if he had, he would
have been brilliant. He was brilliant at everything.

Silence.

WOMAN
You should come to the park with me sometime. We
can sit on the bench and eat ice-cream.

MAN
I…don't go out much…

WOMAN

Oh, but I mean you could, if you wanted to? I mean you can walk and everything?

MAN

Walk? I can dance.

But I don't really like going out…

WOMAN

You stay inside all day?

MAN

I have a fantastic view of the car park here…watch everyone going to Checkers. The other day I saw a man and woman with two trolleys, one filled with meat and the other with toilet paper – now what does that say to you? In here, out there.

WOMAN (*Laughing.*)

Oh, I just thought…you know, an ice-cream…

MAN

We can eat ice-cream here. I'll ask Skrewf, I'm sure he has contacts.

WOMAN

Ok.

She gives him the biscuits.

MAN

No, you and your mom – for after supper.

WOMAN

Thank you.

>   *Silence.*
>   *She kisses him full on the mouth.*
>   *Pause.*
>   *She fumbles with the door – evolving into a door*
>   *dance, simple and delicate.*
>   *She exits.*
>   *He is shaken – struck by the kiss.*
>   *He polishes his shoes.*
>   *Cross-fade.*

WOMAN

So I'm busy painting her nails and she is delirious
from the morphine and she says to me, 'Aren't you
a lucky girl…I bought you a snack-which-maker for
your birthday…a white one.' First of all it's not my
birthday, and secondly she hasn't been out in over a
year.

MAN

Maybe she sent Skrewf!

WOMAN (*Laughs.*)

My Mom and Skrewf! That's a thought.

MAN

What is a snack-which-maker?

WOMAN

Makes toasted sandwiches, they were popular years ago? Have you never had one?

MAN

No. But I know how to make bioscope egg.

Tidying up, she opens the desk top.

Don't do that! Leave that alone.

WOMAN

It's fine I was just…

MAN

No, not there.

WOMAN

Ok…ok. What, are you hiding something? Some hidden treasure? Did you rob a bank?

MAN

It's just personal stuff!

WOMAN

Ok.

Silence.

Did I tell you about number thirty-six?

MAN
No.

WOMAN
She and twenty-four.

MAN
You're joking! Twenty-four. And what about him?

WOMAN
Twenty-six told me he has been doing it with forty-four for seven years and she didn't know.

MAN
I wouldn't do it with forty-four even with seventeen's penis!

WOMAN
Come on she's not that bad!

MAN
Have you heard her voice? Sounds like a car alarm... Harryyyyyyyyyyy!

WOMAN
Do you think I should open a little shop... You know when my mother...you know?

MAN
Kicks the bucket?

She helps him change his trousers.

WOMAN
Ja. I've been thinking about a candle shop. When my aunt stayed with us on the farm. She made her own candles. All shapes and colors. Candles in the shape of cows and sheep. Once she even made a small doll which she said looked exactly like me.

MAN
Where is it now? The candle.

WOMAN
I left it at the farmhouse, on my window-sill. I once lit it, but only for a few seconds – couldn't bear the thought of it melting.

MAN
Do you think you will ever go back? To the farm, I mean?

WOMAN
Maybe. I always thought we were lonely on the farm, that's until we came to the city. Then I realized that to be lonely in an open field with the horizon far far in the distance, is not lonely at all, just very quiet.

Anyway there is no one left there now, just my older brother and his wife.

That's why I was thinking of the shop. Keep me going.

MAN

I think it's a good idea.

WOMAN

Really? My Mom says it's a silly dream. It would close in a month.

MAN

Rubbish. It's brilliant! I think you should do it. You could sell books as well.

WOMAN

Sure I'll sell all your books.

They laugh.

I was thinking…

I was thinking that… I think I love you.

You know it's fine now…we're allowed…to… And I think I do.

He picks up a book.

You don't have to say anything…I mean it's ok. Ok?

MAN

Ok.

Music.

Cross-fade.

The MAN is fussing with his books. The WOMAN is looking out of the window.

MAN

Certainty, certainty, certainty, certainty, if you say
the word enough times, it loses its meaning…

WOMAN

The concrete looks so grey.

MAN

Because it is. For a while anyway!

WOMAN

And when it's dry – light white. She is going to die
soon.

MAN

There comes that arsehole!

WOMAN

She says that she wants her ashes to be scattered in
the duck-pond. She says the only time she ever feels
at peace is when she is watching the ducks.

You're not listening to me?

MAN

I heard, she wants to be scattered with the ducks.

WOMAN

You know sometimes you remind me of her. She
also never listens.

MAN
Hey! Voetsak!

WOMAN
What have you got against the poor guy anyway?

MAN
He lies!

WOMAN
How do you know?

MAN
'Ag sorry my mother, I mean my grandmother's
brother's got a coma, and he needs a vaccination,
her cousin threw a dart in the back of her head,
when she was twelve, but now it's gone sceptic
'cause she's thirty-seven and the doctor was away
on holiday, that's why she couldn't have a tetanus
injection so can I please have five bob?'

WOMAN (*Laughing.*)
Maybe we should get a dog?

MAN
My dad was always good with dogs.

WOMAN
How come whenever I want to talk about my
mother, we talk about your father instead?

MAN
We know your mother is dying.

WOMAN
And we know your father was an arsehole.

MAN
Not always! He was very strong, we were all scared
of him…

WOMAN
I'm scared of you.

MAN
You're scared of everyone.

WOMAN
I know.

Pause.

MAN
Marry me.

WOMAN
What?

MAN
Marry me.

WOMAN

What are you talking about marriage, I… We don't
even…

MAN

Shhhh there's silence, the chapel's full on both sides.
Look! Flowers everywhere, you're standing at the
end of the aisle in white lace – you look beautiful
– daisies in your hair, you're shaking – trembling
– have you overdone the lipstick? Do you have
enough eye shadow? You're slightly out of breath,
mustn't faint now. The padre winks at the organist…
Shhhhhh shhhhhhhhhhh. Seventy-seven years old,
she does a double-take, not sure, she winks again da
da da da da deee da…

Do you Elizabeth Meyor take Jan Abrahms to be
your lawfully wedded husband?

WOMAN

I do.

MAN

Will you put up with his snoring, his cranky jokes,
his belching and farting for the next thirty-five years?

WOMAN

I will.

MAN

Your turn, come on…

WOMAN
Will you Jan Abrahams take Elsie to be your lawfully wedded wife?

MAN
I will.

WOMAN
Will you take her for a walk everyday to the duck-pond?

MAN
I will.

WOMAN
Will you buy her a snowflake ice-cream on each occasion?

MAN
I will.

WOMAN
Will you…

MAN (*Distracted, looking out window.*)
Hey Skrewf! Get me some atcha! Two tins! Ja Brew, nou ne?

> *She tidies up, packing books into the desk, as she does so she finds an envelope.*

She looks at the address, turns it round. She is puzzled.
She folds it in half and tucks it into her pocket.

WOMAN
I must go.

MAN
Don't go yet.

WOMAN
I have to, she's watching the clock. Finish your book
and I'll be back soon.

Music.

Cross-fade.

MAN picks up the window and looks out.

WOMAN
'Stand up!' cried his father. But he couldn't stand
up. Time passed and as his legs grew weaker and
weaker, his father grew more and more angry. And
his father's anger made him frightened.

MAN
For months I looked sideways at the dinner table,
hid in my room, avoided him in the passage. Then
one day I was on the toilet, he came in to wash
his face. He didn't see me. He opened the tap and
worked the soap all over his face.

I can still hear the cries Dad, they are getting louder…

He spun round and glared at me.

'You hear nothing, do you hear me? You hear nothing!'

I looked at the running water and knew he was lying. All the fathers were lying.

WOMAN

The woman hates this story. She has heard it too often.

Cross-fade.

MAN

Ah please! Get a life!

WOMAN

I've had enough. I'm getting sick, my skin is crawling, small gogas all over me. And when I wake up and look in the mirror, there's nothing there.

MAN

You mean you're not there, or the gogas aren't there?

WOMAN

The gogas. The gogos!

MAN

And you're saying your gogos are my fault?

WOMAN

I'm just saying…I have had enough.

MAN

Would you like me to kill myself?

WOMAN

Sometimes I dream I'm at your funeral.

MAN

Do you see me in the coffin?

WOMAN

No, I see my mother.

God! I feel so stuck here in this place! It's like burnt
soup, like boiled cabbage, it's suffocating! Can't we
just…can't we just…get out for a while, go for a walk
in the park, eat an ice-cream, like normal people.

MAN

We can eat an ice-cream here, what's wrong with
here?

WOMAN

Here! Here? Here is suffocating, why can't you
come out with me once in a while, help me take Mrs
Smidt's dogs for a walk in the mornings? Get out, get
some fresh air, sunlight, life!

MAN

You call carrying Mrs Smidt's beagle round the park
a walk? A life? Coming up for air? No wonder that
poor dog looks so sad. All the other dogs are pissing
themselves, 'Look at Elfonzo being carried around
by a woman,' I'm surprised he doesn't jump down
and bite you in the arse. Do you think he wants to
be carried around – he's seeing turds going past all
in different states of decay, all coded with different
sorts of information, because a turd on the lawn is
the bloody *Sunday Times* for the dog, that's where he
gets all his information…sniff sniff…

WOMAN

When she died I thought there would be a release.
No more ranting, raving, self-pity, drugs, addiction,
bedsores, overdoses, stomach pumps, green bile.
Changing your parent's nappy is so… There were
times when I just wanted to pick up her nicotine-
stained pillow, and smother her. Make her go away.

MAN

She was brave; she struggled for a long time.

WOMAN

It's hard being a child with a mother who is always
dying.

MAN

Sure, but imagine being her.

Silence.

Tea?

WOMAN

Ja.

MAN

You are an amazing woman. You're going to be ok.
Maybe we should get another dog.

WOMAN

During the last few weeks of her life, she grew this
little beard. I'd never seen it before.

I think she must have shaved it.

Then after she stopped breathing, the nurse said
I could spend some time with her. Clean her up.
Change her night-dress.

There was a bit of blood on her mouth, and I got a
face-cloth to clean it. I thought about making her up,
you know, lipstick, eye-shadow, like in the movies.

She didn't have any panties on, so I took a clean
shiny nylon pair from her bag and lifted her
heavy legs so that I could cover her private area. I
imagined the mortuary men seeing her smoothness
and I felt vomity. Her body was so heavy, filled with
water from the broken kidneys. Her once thin hands,
with long fingers and painted nails, now bloated,
I put on her panties and her gown and made her
decent. And then as I bent to kiss her face, I once

again noticed her beard. I looked in her bag for a
razor, found one and shaved her dead chin.

Silence.

MAN
Good. A woman like that couldn't go to heaven with
a beard.
Pause.
What do you really want?

WOMAN
Want?

MAN
Yes?

She detaches the wooden legs...

WOMAN
As he grew older, his body became weak, he felt
himself sinking into the earth, he felt his family
sinking, the village, the town. He felt the earth hating
them, their rot.

MAN
I felt us sinking like a fly in porridge, like dissolving,
we were being swallowed...God and his blankets.

WOMAN

The woman listens to the story. She knows it well.
She can even tell it, perhaps better than the man.
And when she stops for a moment, when she is still,
she knows it's true. And sometimes she too can hear
the crying.

She can feel herself sinking.

There are many ways of loving.

She loves because she needs to. He doesn't, because
he can't.

Want…

MAN

Yes.

WOMAN

I need to go, I need to leave…

She closes the door, he falls.

*Images – separate from one another: her, sitting
quietly on the door, reading the letter that she found
in his desk; and him, alone reading in bed.*

Time passes.

Lights up on room.

WOMAN enters.

*The MAN is frenetic, troubled, very concerned with
his books.*

He walks over to a small table, lights a cigarette,
looks out the window, reads a book, once again
looks out the window…goes back to his books.

There is a knock on the door.

The MAN provides the door for her entrance, he
opens it, sees her and shuts it angrily.

The WOMAN opens the door.

MAN
Are you back?

WOMAN
Yes.

MAN
For how long?

WOMAN
As long as I can bear it.

MAN
Rather go now.

WOMAN
And leave you alone?

MAN
Yes.

Pause.

WOMAN
Did you wash the pots?

MAN
They're not my pots.

WOMAN
Of course they are your pots.

MAN
You bought them.

WOMAN
Yes. But for your house!
Pause.
Well did you wash them?

MAN
No.

Pause.

WOMAN
And the magazines? Did you read them?

MAN
What for?

WOMAN
For some light entertainment, you can't sit with this crap all day.

MAN

Maybe the owner will come back and take the books. That will make you happy.

WOMAN

You made that up, it's a lie…

MAN

Ja, ja…

WOMAN

And there is no rot, no sinking. You made that up too.

Are you hungry?

MAN

The earth turned slowly to mud…

WOMAN

Another book, another story.

Angrily she throws one of his books across the room.

MAN

Under God's blanket, and then another blanket and another and another…

WOMAN

How did you breathe?

MAN
Periscope pipe.

WOMAN
And now? Where are you now?

MAN
Here.

WOMAN
Above ground?

MAN
Whatever!

WOMAN
Why did it happen?

MAN
I've told you a million times. You just won't listen to
me.
Pause.
Did you scatter her ashes?

WOMAN
Did you know that those hobos have eaten nearly
all the fuckin' ducks? I went there with her ashes this
morning with every intention of scattering them in
the pond, and all I could count was six ducks. There
used to be at least nineteen, I mean what happened
to the others?

MAN
Who am I to you?

WOMAN
Ok, so it was her wish to be scattered in the pond,
but she didn't realize that soon the pond wouldn't
have any ducks. She didn't realize that the ducks
were disappearing nineteen to the dozen. Or did
she? Surely she doesn't want to lie in an ice-cold
dirty duck-pond with no ducks.

MAN
Who am I to you?

WOMAN
What?

MAN
Who am I to you?

WOMAN
Just a man...who is kind and intelligent and...who
has various delusions.

MAN
Delusions?

WOMAN
Well, someone who believes that his town was
trapped underground, and who reads books as if
they were the bible must be delusional.

She loses control and throws one book after another across the room. He scuttles after them.

MAN

So if I believed that my town was trapped above ground, and I read the bible, then I wouldn't be delusional?

WOMAN

You should try read something else for a change, or why don't you get a TV, I'm sure we could organize a portable.

There are all sorts of interesting things for you to watch. Sitcoms, the news, sport.

MAN

What have you got against the books I read?

WOMAN

Nothing, they're all just so depressing.

MAN

You've read them?

WOMAN

Not really, but I know what they are about, they might be fancy literature, but they are not really helpful.

What do you see in them?

MAN

These words are real words, not common old garden words, but tasty sex words, infant-sucking-tit words. When I read these I'm amongst kings, soldiers, bastards, witches, orphans.

WOMAN

Orphans? I know, I found the letter; I've been trying to find the courage to...

MAN

Earth, sand and rock sunk. Contours and dirt roads fell away or sank; stonewalls and trees leant over in the sponge-like earth.

Nobody in the town knew why, or even asked why. But I knew. It was because of the cry. They were being punished for not going to look, for not helping the wounded. I tried to tell my parents; even some of my teachers, but no one would listen. No one could hear...

WOMAN

Jan you were abandoned...

MAN

...Cows and sheep, bleating and bulking, struggled to lift their feet out of the sticky dirty sour stink of sore flesh and people's lies. Father's lies, Mother's biscuits and sweet perfume.

WOMAN
I saw the report.

MAN
The ground was rebelling against them, accusing
them. Was the rot just in our town or was it
everywhere in the world? Was the whole world
sinking into its own filth, its rot, its lies?

WOMAN
How long did you think you could keep it from me?

MAN
The people of the town with all their certainty
wouldn't admit that the earth had turned on its
owners. That they were being punished.

WOMAN
In a brown envelope.
I found it when I was tidying your books,

MAN
(*Becoming more and more agitated as the town sinks.*)
Certainty, confidence, conviction, faith, belief,
assurance, firmness, sureness…
Certainty – cup-cakes, cattle, the certainty of cattle,
farmers, four walls, two eyes and a nose – house,
family, mom, dad, kid. Confusion no not confusion,
certainty is fences, buildings, stones, foundations,

build wall, more walls – isolation. Cocoon, hide-out, dug-out, die!

WOMAN

Didn't they have money or was it just impossible for them to take care of you?

MAN

The boy's father, like other fathers, reinforced the disappearing walls of their house with planks, tins, sheets of glass and plastic against the treason of the earth. Frenzy, extra water-tanks attached to houses and pantries filled with foodstuff and provisions. In full concession that the earth was swallowing the town…

WOMAN

Jan.

MAN

Periscope pipes were welded to roofs, and houses were attached to one another with sewerage pipes.

WOMAN

Come on, it happened, your family deserted you.

MAN

Certainty? Certainty, certainty, certainty, certainty, if you say a word enough times, it loses its meaning. It doesn't mean certainty anymore, you are uncertain

if certain means certain, or if uncertain means not to
be certain.

And then at last the day came, with ropes and beams
and sledges they struggled into the main road, even
I was there, my father carrying me, and my spaghetti
legs dangling in the air.

WOMAN
Jan, this is a lie! It's a lie!

MAN
A lie! A lie! What? The world isn't sinking? I can't
hear the crying? You're a lie!
You're a fuckin' lie! Why don't you just go! Piss off!
Get out!

WOMAN
Jan I…

MAN
Out! Get out ! Get out!

WOMAN
The woman wonders at it all, her need, her
usefulness, is it just going to carry on like this? But
this is not a real love story; no beginning, middle
and end. This is a silkworm thing. Layers and layers
meeting, biographies clashing and being forced
together, tied together. She feels herself swallowed,
she too is underground.

Cross-fade.

The sound.

The instrument.

Ritualistically the MAN buries the wooden legs...

Cross-fade.

The WOMAN sits alone.

The MAN enters.

WOMAN
And now?

MAN
I'm here!

WOMAN
How have you been?

MAN
Dismantled. And you?

WOMAN
Unraveled.

He sits beside her.

MAN
Is was a hot day, we were all crammed into the old
Ford. We stopped off at a petrol station, the petrol
attendant was smoking and I wondered if he was
going to set the car alight. Mom got out and bought

us soft-serve ice-creams. I should have known then, she had never bought us ice-creams before. Then we headed off on a long road and I fell asleep in the car. When I woke up I saw stairs, banisters, a shiny floor, my father was carrying me, he put me down on a bench, my fingers curled around the wooden slats and then a lady joined us. Father sat down next to me, I remember the ridges in his brown corduroy trousers, he took a book from inside his jacket and said I could have it, said that when I had finished reading it he would be back to fetch me. He squeezed my shoulders together and left.

WOMAN
And he never came back?

MAN
I read the book; when I finished, I waited at the window of my dormitory. He didn't come so I thought that perhaps I'd missed something, maybe I hadn't read it carefully enough. I read it again, savouring each word. I slowed down when I got to the last chapter, thinking that I should give him time, what if he had run out of petrol? Or what if he had had a puncture? I listened for the sound of the car wheels on the gravel outside. I read the last line very very slowly and went to the window.

WOMAN
And then you read other books, hundreds of books.

Silence.

MAN

Did you get rid of the ashes?

WOMAN

Yes today!

But not in the pond, I just couldn't. There is this old Jacaranda tree just next to the pond. It looks like a cradle with four arms stretching outwards. Funny thing is that it still has its blossoms. December and still purple. I rubbed her ashes into the dry bark. It felt right.

MAN

How many ducks?

WOMAN

Three.

MAN laughs softly.

The town did sink.

MAN

Yes.

WOMAN

And you did hear a cry. You still hear a cry.

MAN

Yes.

WOMAN
Is that the whole story? Have you told me
everything now?

MAN
I think so.

WOMAN
Is there more?

MAN
There is always more!

Lights fade.

For information on these and other plays and books
published by Oberon, or for a free catalogue, listing all
titles and cast breakdowns, visit our website

www.oberonbooks.com

info@oberonbooks.com • 020 7607 3637